This book is dedicated to all the children in my life.
You inspire me, make me laugh, make me strong and
make me feel loved. It is for all of you that I
do what I do.

—♡ E.G.S.

Thank you to all the people who have believed in
and inspired me on this long journey towards
betterment and improving my skillset.
You're the inspiration that keeps me
painting and illustrating.

—L.V.

WEIRD WENDELL

A book about tolerance, acceptance, friendship, and being okay with being different.

Another great book in the
Ms. Ellen's Got Swag Collection

Written by E.G. Sparer
Illustrations by Luke Valentine

CONTENTS

THE GREAT FIDGET SPINNER ROBBERY

It happened again, this is the second time this

week that Big Mike stole my stuff.

First my lunch with my favorite hot chips

and left over halloween candy.

And then, today, he stole my favorite fidget spinner,

the one with the gold trim that goes super fast.

I was in the snack bar, spinning it on my nose,

looking seriously cool, when out of nowhere,

Big Mike walked over, and with his big dirty hand,

just slapped it off my nose.

"Gimme that, git!" he said.

I'm not sure, but I think I screamed like a little baby. I could hear kids laughing.

Now I don't know if you have ever gotten hit in the nose, but it hurts really, really bad. I could feel my nose swelling and tried to hold back the tears. I looked around the snack bar.

Kids were looking at me; some were laughing.

Here I was again, Weird Wendell being laughed

at. I was getting madder and madder.

I felt like my brain might explode,

but then something happened.

Something weird and wonderful happened!

SCRATCH

I am Wendell D. Worthington, the 3rd.

Sounds pretty important right?

Funny thing is, I never met Wendell D. Worthington the 1st, and barely know Wendell D. Worthington the 2nd. Weird right? But here I am,

Wendell D. Worthington the 3rd.

But most people just call me

"Weird Wendell."

I am currently in the fourth grade.

Fourth grade is way harder then third.

And it's not just the math.

Especially if you are really

small for your age.

Mom says I will have a growth spurt soon.

I'm not sure what this is, but it sounds kinda messy.

As for being called weird,

well, I guess you could

say I'm a little weird.

Since I've been a baby I've

always had a lot to worry about.

For one thing, I scratch… a lot. I scratch

because I have this stupid thing called Eczema.

It makes my skin really itchy.

Every picture of me as a baby,

I am scratching some part of my body.

It's just who I am.

Like if someone bites their nails all the time

or taps their pencil all the time,

I scratch all the time.

Sometimes my face gets so itchy

that I can't stop scratching

and I make my face bleed.

This might look cool on Halloween,

but most days it's just really annoying.

Some kids tease me and call me "Scratch,"

and lots of other names.

But I don't care because it makes me different,

and for some reason I like being different.

It feels kinda right for me.

So like I said, I'm pretty weird.

BERNIE

I live with my mom, Bernadette.

Some people call her Bernie.

My mom told me once that her name means

strong and brave as a bear.

I like that, and it's true, she really is brave.

I watched her pick up a spider

in our kitchen with her bare hands.

I think it was a black widow. If it bites you,

you might die. As far as I'm concerned,

we're all lucky to be alive!

And mom takes really good care of me,

the only thing is, she worries too much.

I tell her, "Mom! Calm down, I'm ok!"

She worries about my itching and scratching.

Oh, and she hates video games, she says if you play

them too much they literally fry your brain.

I tell her, "Mom, I'll have one fried brain

with a side of fries, please."

She rolls her eyes at me and laughs.

I like to make mom laugh.

One thing I do kinda hate is that

she has to work so hard.

Mom works long hours at the thrift store.

A thrift store is where people bring their

old things they don't want anymore; clothes,

furniture, all kinds of stuff.

So this is where I get all my clothes from.

Now this may sound like a bad thing,

but one time I found a 20 dollar bill in the

pocket of a pair of jeans my mom brought home.

Mom, Westley, and I had a big pepperoni pizza that

night and chocolate chip ice cream afterwards.

Keep those old clothes coming mom!

Oh, and Westley is my little brother.

He's just 2 years old, but he's super smart.

He is really my half-brother

because we have the same mom but different dads.

But I don't think of him as half a brother.

I think of him as my whole brother.

Plus, he's really funny. He likes to throw his peas

and carrots at me.

Westley hates peas and carrots.

So I guess you are wondering about my Dad,

Wendell D. Worthington the 2nd.

He's usually not around.

I'm not sure where he lives because

I haven't seen him in a long time. People ask me

about him, but I really don't know much.

I usually tell them he is a fisherman in Alaska.

Kids think this is cool, so thats my story.

I mean he could be a fisherman in Alaska, right?

He sent me a card on my birthday one year

and said he'd see me soon. I waited by the window

for 2 weeks every night. I guess soon hasn't come

yet.

My mom and Wendell D. Worthington the 2nd

never got married. The only thing they had in

common was one little itchy boy. That would be me.

They argued a lot and then dad left.

Then mom got a boyfriend named Stanley Stanley.

Yes, Stanley Stanley, first name and

last name the same.

Weird right? What was Mrs. Stanley thinking

thinking when she named her son Stanley Stanley?

So, Bernadette and Stanley Stanley

had my little brother Westley, then they started

arguing a lot so Stanley Stanley left.

I said "Goodbye goodbye, Stanley Stanley."

So it's just me, mom and Westley,

which is just the way I like it.

I miss Wendell D. Worthington the 2nd sometimes,

but most days I'm too busy to think about it.

Ya know with the scratching and stuff.

STEFANO

My favorite person in the whole world,

is my best friend Stefano. He is from Venezuela.

Stefano and I have been friends since he

came to my school.

We can tell each other anything. I can even cry in

front of him and he never laughs and he never

makes fun of my itching.

He says, "Lo siento tu picazon (Sorry you're itchy)."

When you say his name, Stefano, you
have to pronounce it STEF-FON-O.
Some of the mean kids call him Stew-pid-doe
(stupido), but he doesn't care. Although, I'm not
sure he understands this is an insult, because his
English is not so great. So he just laughs.
Stefano speaks a mixture of Spanish and English,
some people call it Spanglish. I call it cool!

Stefano has 2 sisters and 2 brothers and a fat dog
named Gordito.
They feed him tamales, I think.

Stefano is kind of weird like me, thats why I like him. He dresses really cool. He only wears soccer shirts. That's his favorite thing. He can do anything with a soccer ball. He can even balance it on his head.

Also Stefano is super smart and knows everything about animals.

He can tell you what the biggest, fastest, smartest, animals are and anything else you want to know about them. He told me once a snail can sleep for three years, and that elephants are the only animals that can't jump. Oh, and squirrels can't burp or vomit. I'm not sure if this is a good thing or bad thing. Oh, and he also told me, a giraffe's tongue is so long, that he uses it to clean his ears. Now thats just gross.

Not only is Stefano smart, but he is very brave and when the kids tease me about being short or about my scratching he stands up for me in English and Spanish. Muchas Gracias Stefano (Thank you very much)!

BIG MIKE: AKA THE BULLY

One of the worst kids in the whole school,

maybe the whole world, is BIG Mike. They call him

Big Mike cause well, he's really big…like 6th grade

big, but he is only in 4th grade.

Hmmm…wonder why.

Big Mike is as mean as they come. He will take

your money, your lunch, your homework and what-

ever else he wants.

And for some crazy reason he always wears

these big, old, dirty brown cowboy boots. I may not be a genius, but I am pretty sure he is not a real cowboy.

Mom says kids who bully other kids are unhappy inside. She says we should feel sorry for them. But hey, who's feeling sorry for me when he swipes my lunch with my favorite cookies?

Oh, and get this, Big Mike's favorite past time is picking his nose. He does it on the school bus, he does it in gym class and he does it in the snack bar.

They say three girls threw up last year watching him

pick his nose and eat an egg salad sandwich

all at the same time.

Stefano says Big Mike is "asqueroso" (disgusting).

I agree. Yuk!

SUPER WENDELL

Ok, so back to the part about Big Mike and the

weird wonderful thing that happened. Ok, so after

Big Mike took my fidget spinner,

I started getting madder and madder,

I felt like my head might explode!

Then something happened, something

weird and wonderful happened!

I felt my body changing, I ran into the

boys room as fast as I could. I started feeling strange

and a little scared. I leaned against the wall.

My whole body was shaking. I could

feel my blood rushing through my veins.

I could feel my muscles tingling, they felt like they

were getting bigger. I could feel my body growing.

I felt taller and stronger! I looked in the mirror.

I was taller!

I could barely see my face in the mirror.

I had to bend over to see myself. My face had no

scabs on it and I wasn't itchy anymore. I was

completely transformed. I'm not sure how this

happened, but I'm really liking it!

I didn't look like Wendell D. Worthington the

3rd or Weird Wendell.

I looked like SUPER Wendell, a tall strong kid with

clear skin.

I left the bathroom feeling brave and strong.

I walked into the snack bar with my shoulders back

and my head held high.

Everyone turned around to see me. I heard gasps and

someone yelled, "Who is that?"

Stefano yelled, "That's Super Wendell, mi mejor

amigo (my best friend)!"

There was Big Mike, sitting at my table,

egg salad dripping from his lips, spinning MY fidget

spinner. I walked over in my new tall strong body.

"Excuse me," I said, in a deep voice that I didn't even recognize. "I believe that fidget spinner is mine!"

Big Mike looked surprised and confused. I grabbed it out of his dirty little hands. Then something crazy happened. I reached down with my big strong arms and picked up Big Mike by the cowboy boots and threw him across the snack bar. Yikes! How did I do that???

He landed on a lunch table right into a plate of mashed potatoes. Whoa!

I walked over to Big Mike, looked at his mashed potato face, and said "Thank you very much."

"Yeah… Muchas gracias!" said Stefano. Big Mike looked up from the table I could see the mashed potatoes up his nose. I knew he'd be picking potatoes out of his nose real soon. Big Mike looked shocked. I took my fidget spinner and started walking out of the snack bar. I couldn't see behind me but I know everyone was looking at me.

As I walked, my muscles started tingling.

I could actually feel my legs shrinking, and my skin

began to itch. I didn't have to look in the mirror.

I knew I was back to my short itchy self. I was

Weird Wendell again.

WHAT JUST HAPPENED?

Stefano followed me into the bathroom.

I was leaning against the wall sweating.

My face was super itchy and my muscles ached.

"Lo que acaba de suceder (What just

happened)?" said Stefano.

"I don't know," I said. I think I turned into

a super human or something.

"Do you know what you did?" said Stefano.

"You threw Big Mike across the room.

It was awesome! You, Weird Wendell,

threw the biggest, meanest, worstest bully in whole

school across the snack bar."

"I know!" I said. "But, I don't know how

I did it. I just know when Big Mike made me mad, I

could feel something happening to me. My muscles

started tingling and I could feel my legs growing and

I felt super strong. It was like a dream or a miracle

or something. My mom always says I'm special…

Maybe this is what she meant!"

HEATHER

Heather was the prettiest girl in school;

and even though she was pretty and smart,

Heather was nice to everyone, even Big Mike.

I really like Heather, just like every other boy in the

4th grade. But she would never be interested in me,

a short itchy boy, who everyone thinks is weird.

Actually, one time Heather said she liked my

shirt. I wore it everyday for 3 months. I don't know

what happened to it, I think mom threw it away. It

got kinda of dirty and smelled like hot dogs.

Stefano says he sees Heather looking at me and thinks she likes me, but I don't know if she likes me or likes me likes me. I think we are friends, but I don't want to get stuck in the friend zone, if ya know what I mean.

One time Big Mike was teasing me about my itching and Heather walked over. She tapped Big Mike on the shoulder.

"Hey," she said, "Why don't you pick on somebody your own size."

Big Mike just looked at her and flashed his evil grin, "Oooohhhh," said Big Mike.

"Is SCRATCH your boyfriend? Do you love the itchy boy?"

Heather just gave him a mean stare and said, "You better leave him alone or I'll tell everyone you still wet the bed."

"Yeah!" said Stefano with a big grin. "Tú cama grande mojado (You big bed wetter)."

Big Mike's face turned beet red, he turned towards me, he was just about to hit me, but stopped suddenly.

Mr. Jingles, the science teacher, came walking down the hallway. Mr. Jingles is not his real name. It's Mr. Simpson but he always has keys in his pocket and he jingles them when he walks, so everyone calls him Mr. Jingles.

Big Mike looked at me with his evil face.

"I'll get you later, git!" And he stomped away in his dirty brown cowboy boots.

I looked at Heather. "Thanks," I said. She just smiled and walked away.

"What a girl," I thought. "What a girl!"

THE DANCE

Every year our school puts on a fall dance. I have never gone, but I think I'm a good dancer, if I say so myself. When no one is around, I like to dance in the mirror. One time my little brother Westley saw me and started doing his own little crazy dance. I cracked up.

That little guy is hilarious!

This year's theme for the dance is "Superheroes."

Everyone is supposed to dress up as a superhero.

After what happened the other day in the snack bar, this might work out perfect.

But you know what would really be perfect?

If Heather would dance with me.

Maybe if this happens, she can see that I'm a good dancer and like me, like me and we could get out of the friend zone.

Mom says girls like boys who can dance.

Apparently, Wendell D. Worthington the 2nd, was a really good dancer. Mom liked this.

The day of the dance finally came. I felt so nervous, I couldn't even eat my waffles this morning. This made my brother Westley happy because he loves waffles. I told him he could have mine. He pulled them off my plate, ate one, and threw the other at the TV, just missing mom.

I decided to wear my Super Frog Man Halloween costume to the dance. It was a little small, and it had a candy corn stuck to the mask (which I took off and ate), but I think I looked ok.

Stefano said he would meet me there. He is coming as the Spanish superhero, Gato de Fuego (Firecat). I didn't know much about this Gato guy, but Stefano says he has mucho super powers. He says Gato de Fuego has superhuman speed, can crawl walls and is a fighting pro.

He is also highly intelligent and can speak two languages. And when Gato de Fuego is not busy saving the world, he is playing soccer. Sounds like the perfect costume for Stefano.

A REAL HERO!

I walked into the gym. Whoa! It looked like a comic book threw up in here. There were red, white and blue streamers and balloons everywhere. Someone had tried really hard to make the gym look pretty, but it still kinda smelled like dirty socks.

There was a table set up with a big punch bowl. It was filled with something that looked like green slush. If you looked closer you could see someone had put some gummy worms in the punch.

I definitely wanted some of that!

There were cookies and cupcakes decorated with superheroes and someone made a big banner that read "Superhero Dance." It was falling off the wall and Mr. Jingles was trying to tape it back up.

There was music playing and a few kids were dancing. Most kids were just standing around talking, looking like they didn't know why they were there. The girls were on one side of the gym and the boys were on the other.
A couple of kids found a soccer ball and were kicking it in the corner.

Miss Baron the Spanish teacher was wearing a

red shirt that said "Soy un superheroe"

(I am a superhero).

Nice costume Señorita Baron.

It was suppose to be a "Superhero Dance" but some

kids were wearing other kinds of costumes.

There was one kid wearing a really scary zombie

mask chasing a couple girls. They were screaming,

"HELP, HELP!!!"

I don't think they really needed help and

zombies aren't superheroes. Oh well.

I need to find Stefano. He was coming as

Gato de Fuego (Firecat), so I guess I need to

look for a superhero cat. I started walking

around and then… I saw her!

VALOROUS AKA HEATHER

There she was!

It was Heather, dressed as Valorous,

the beautiful, superhero from the planet Stalwart.

Valorous is a character from a video game called

Crystal Palace. It's very popular with the girls be-

cause there are princesses and castles and unicorns,

ya know stuff girls love. In order to get power,

you have to solve puzzles and then you are

rewarded with crystals.

Once you have a certain amount of crystals

you can buy diamond rings and horses and clothes, and all kinds of girl stuff. A lot of girls love to play this game, plus it's not violent and that makes their parents happy.

Heather looked super pretty. Her hair was tied back with a blue ribbon. She was wearing a long purple and pink gown with sequins that were shimmering under the gym lights.

On her head she had beautiful crown.

Wow!!! She really did look like a princess.

Heather was standing by herself, just looking around.

All of a sudden I felt like I couldn't breathe. It might have been my mask. It smelled like sweat and it was making me feel really hot. My face was starting to itch under the mask and I could feel my legs shaking.

Why was I so nervous? And where was Stefano?

Someone tapped me on my shoulder. Hey? What? I turned around, it was Stefano.

"I am Gato de Fruego, the bravest cat in the universe!" he said with a big grin. Stefano's face was painted with whiskers and a pink nose.

I laughed, "You look so funny," I said.

"I am not funny!" said Stefano.

"I am MUY VALIENTE (very brave)!"

"Okay, yes. You are muy valiente," I said.

"Hey, did you see who is here?" said Stefano

"You mean Heather?" I said.

"Yes," said Stefano. "I just saw her when I came in. She looks muy bonita (very pretty)."

"Yea," I said. "I know. I want to go and talk to her, but my legs are shaking and my face is itching under my mask."

"Boy," I said. "This would be a great time for me to turn into Super Wendell! But I don't know how I did it the first time. It just kinda happened when I got really really mad.

I bet if I was Super Wendell, Heather would definitely want to dance with me.

Maybe if I wish really really hard… I wanna be Super Wendell..I wanna be Super Wendell…I wanna be Super Wendell… please make me Super Wendell!"

"Thats enough," said Stefano. "No mas (no more). You are great just as Wendell. Heather likes you. I see her looking at you. You need to ask her to dance, mi amigo. You can do this! Remember, you are the very brave Super Frog Man. So just hop your little frog body over there."

"Oh very funny," I said. Stefano grinned one of his goofy grins.

"Come on, dude. You can do this!"

YOU CAN DO THIS!

"Okay, I can do this!" I said to myself. "I can do this!"

Just as I got the nerve to walk over to Heather, in walked Big Mike.

Of course he would come in right now!

Apparently his superhero costume is a ripped smiley-face T-shirt and dirty brown cowboy boots. What a surprise!

Wait one minute!.. Where was he going? Seriously?

He was heading right over to Heather. My Heather!

As he walked past us, Big Mike gave us one of his mean stares, and with his big dirty hands pushed me and Stefano right into the wall.

"Out of my way you creeps!" he said.

I looked at Stefano. I never saw him this mad. He went up to Big Mike, got right in his face, and with his whiskers and little pink nose yelled,

"Hola pequeño bebé (Hello little baby)! Did you wet your little baby bed last night???"

Yikes, did he just say that to Big Mike?!

My mouth dropped wide open, I stood there

watching Stefano, that boy is really brave, but I'm

thinking, "This can't end well."

Heather just stood there watching.

I didn't know what she was thinking.

But I knew what I was thinking. I was thinking, "I

am soooo itchy."

I lifted my mask so I could scratch a little,

but a little wasn't enough. I kept scratching my face.

It felt so good. And then I looked at my hands. They

were all bloody.

I quickly wiped them on my pants, hoping no one

noticed.

I was still thinking about my bloody face and I started feeling weak and my legs started shaking like a big bowl of jelly. Why would Heather want to dance with me now?

Meanwhile Big Mike and Stefano were still at it. Big Mike got right up in Stefano's face,

"Hey Stupido! Beat it before I smash in your little cat face!" he said.

"MEOW!" Yelled Stefano, right in Big Mike's face.

Mr. Jingles must have seen something going on and quickly came running over. You could hear the jingling from across the room. Big Mike must have seen Mr. Jingles coming and the big baby ran the other way. I just stood there sweating and itching under my frog mask looking at Heather.

I looked at Stefano.

He whispered to me, "Ask her to dance! Go ahead!"

I started to walk over to Heather, when all of a sudden, out of nowhere, came Big Mike. He walked right up to Heather.

SUPER WENDELL TO THE RESCUE

"Come on girl!" he said, and grabbed her arm.

"You know you wanna dance with me!"

Heather pulled her arm away. "Leave me alone!"

she said, and tried to push him away.

I was getting really really mad!

I had to do something.

"Hey," I yelled. "Leave her alone!"

I felt like the world stopped and

everyone was looking at me.

Big Mike turned around, and flashed his evil grin

again. He walked over and grabbed me

by the front of my Super Frog Man costume.

His face was right in my Super Frog Man mask.

I could smell the egg salad on his breath.

"What did you say, little itchy boy???"

Oh, I guess he figured out it was me under the frog

mask. A short boy scratching must have been a clue.

"Come on what ya gonna do, git..huh?"

Then with his gross dirty hand, Big Mike pulled

off my frog mask.

Someone gasped, "Ewwww, he's all bloody!"

"His face is bleeding!" said a girl dressed like a werewolf.

Big Mike started laughing, "Look at the little itchy boy. He's a monster, he doesn't need a mask, his face is ugly enough. He's a little bloody monster!"

My heart dropped, I could feel tears starting to well up. I looked around the gym, some kids were laughing. A few girls were making gagging faces. Stefano was glaring at Big Mike waving his fist and shouting something in Spanish.

"Tú gran tonto (You big dummy)!"

I looked over at Heather, she looked so sad,

like she felt sorry for me. I don't think I ever felt this

sad and embarrassed.

It was the worst feeling ever.

I just wanted to disappear into nowhere.

I started to feel sick to my stomach,

I knew I had to leave.

I started to run to the bathroom.

As I started running,

my body started feeling weird again.

My muscles started tingling.

That weird and wonderful

feeling was happening again! I could feel it!

I could feel the blood rushing into my veins!

My arms were getting bigger and stronger.

I could feel myself growing,

my legs were getting longer,

 and my face wasn't itchy anymore. I wasn't Weird

Wendell anymore,

I was Super Wendell!!!

 I bent down to look in the mirror,

yup no scabs,

strong arms, tall guy…

that's me, Super Wendell!

And right now I have some important business to

take care of!

WANT SOME PUNCH

I walked back into the gym. I felt great.

I was tall and strong again!

And now I was looking for Big Mike!

Stefano saw me walking in.

He yelled, "Look! It's the amazing

Super Wendell!"

Big Mike turned around and his face went white.

"Oh no! Not again!" Big Mike said.

He tried to run, but I just reached out and

grabbed him by his smiley t-shirt.

Stefano yelled, "He looks thirsty, Wendell! Don't you think he looks thirsty?"

"Yeah," I said. "He does! Come on, Big Mike. Let's go get you some punch."

I carried Big Mike by the front of his shirt over to the punch bowl and put his big face right into the green slush. I pulled him out.

He had a gummy worm up his nose.

"Taste good, baby boy?" said Stefano "Now don't wet your baby bed tonight."

I dropped big Mike right there on the floor. He got up and started backing away.

"I'll get you itchy boy. You better watch out! This is not the end!"

Stefano gave him a look and meowed loudly! "MEOOOOOW!"

Big Mike ran off in his big dirty cowboy boots. I looked at Heather. She smiled at me.

"Thank you, Wendell" she said. "What you did was very brave."

"Yeah, that was Muy valiente!" said Stefano

"Ask her now," whispered Stefano.

"Go ahead! do it."

"Ummm …Heather would you…I mean do you think…um…maybe you would dance with me..I mean if you don't want to…

 I understand..and….uhh."

Heather interrupted me.

"Wendell!" She said, as she looked me right in the eyes.

"Yes! Yes, I would like to dance with you."

My heart skipped a beat. I took Heather's hand and we walked out to the dance floor.

A slow song came on and we started dancing.

I felt so happy, I had never felt this happy before.

Here I was, Weird Wendell, dancing with Heather

the nicest girl in the whole school.

Everyone was watching us, but in a good way.

Not because I was weird or I was itching.

I was just imagining what it would be like to have

Heather as my girlfriend, when all of a sudden,

the lights started flickering. Some girls started

screaming and then all at once the

gym went pitch black!

What was happening?

A LITTLE BACKSTORY...

This is the story of Ellen Sparer, the author, and Luke Valentine, the illustrator.

Once upon a time, Luke lived across the street from Ellen Sparer. Ellen's son, A.J., and Luke became best friends at the age of four. Luke liked to come to A.J.'s house and paint and color with A.J. and his mom, Ellen. Unfortunately, soon after, Luke moved away.

Fast forward twenty years. Ellen is looking for an illustrator, and her son, A.J., tells her to look up Luke Valentine online; he's an amazing artist.

Ellen writes to Luke, "You probably don't remember me. I'm A.J.'s mom. I am writing books and I'm looking for an illustrator."

Luke replies, "Of course I remember you, Ellen. I remember all your art! That's part of what inspired me to become an artist."

And now we're on book six!

And the rest is history!